THE MOTHER PLANE

Secretarius MEMPS Publication

THE MOTHER PLANE

BY
ELIJAH MUHAMMAD
MESSENGER OF ALLAH

Compiled & Edited by
Nasir Makr Hakim
Minister of Elijah Muhammad, Messenger of Allah

Published by
Secretarius MEMPS Publications
111 E Dunlap Ave, Ste 1-217
Phoenix, Arizona 85020-7802
Phone & Fax 602 466-7347
Email: secmemps@gmail.com
Web: www.memps.com

The Mother Plane

Copyright © 1992
Secretarius MEMPS Publications
First Printing 1992
Second Printing 1995
Third Printing 2002
Forth Printing 2004

All rights reserved.
No part of this book may be reproduced
in any form, except for the inclusion of
brief quotations in reviews, without
permission in writing from the
author/publisher.

ISBN10# 1-884855-89-X
EAN13# 978-1-884855-89-4

Printed in the United States of America

TABLE OF CONTENT

TABLE OF CONTENT iv
ACKNOWLEDGEMENT v
EZEKIEL'S WHEEL: MOTHER PLANE 1
EZEKIEL'S WHEEL BATTLE IN THE SKY! 5
THE END OF THE WAR 7
OH WHEEL PART I Messenger Muhammad's
ANALYSIS OF EZEKIEL'S WHEEL 11
O WHEEL Part II Messenger Muhammad's
Analysis of Ezekiel's wheel 15
O Wheel MOTHER OF PLANES Ezekiel's Wheel Part III 19
THE NOISE OF THE WHEEL Part IV
Messenger Muhammad's Analysis of Ezekiel's Wheel 23
INSIDE EZEKIEL'S WHEEL Part V 25
BATTLE IN THE SKY IS NEAR 31
THE GREAT DECISIVE BATTLE IN THE SKY 35
THE BATTLE IN THE SKY 39
THE MOTHER PLANE 41
EZEKIEL'S PROPHECY OF THE WHEEL 45

ACKNOWLEDGEMENT

We seek the assistance of Allah (God), Who came in the person of Master Fard Muhammad, through His Last and Greatest Messenger, the Most Honorable Elijah Muhammad.

We can never thank Allah and His Messenger enough for the Supreme Wisdom, which has been showered upon us, and as the Messenger himself stated, "He (Allah) gave it to me like a flowing fountain. The fountain has enough drink in it to give everyone drink who comes to drink. You don't need a new fountain, just try and drink up what this fountain has."

We therefore avail ourselves of that water without hesitation, because we never get full. This means that the need for another fountain is totally unnecessary.

I would like to thank the Hakim family, Rose, Dur're, Taqqee, Junaid and Khalfani and brother Azzam Waathiq Basit for their hard work and contribution towards making this work of the Messenger accessible to our people.

May Allah, Master Fard Muhammad, continue to bless our continued effort and labor.

As-Salaam-Alaikum

Nasir Makr Hakim, Founder, SECRETARIUS MEMPS

INTRODUCTION

"Today, the wickedness of this civilization has become so great and fair-seeming to the original people of the earth. He [Allah, (God) Master Fard Muhammad] said that twelve leaders from Islam from all over the planet earth have conferred in the root of civilization at Mecca and have found this people disagreeable to live with in peace, and they decided that they must be removed from the planet earth. And the main obstacle that stands in the way of this removal is the so-called Negroes of America who have been lost from the knowledge of self, their God, their religion and the knowledge of the enemy who has robbed them. They must return to their own."

"A Messenger has been sent to teach them the knowledge of self that will qualify them to return to their own. The time of this spreading of the true knowledge of self, God, and devil is the important mission that I (Elijah Muhammad, Last Messenger of Allah) have. As it is written, the life of this world has been made so fair-seeming to you that you cannot conceive of another world that might be better. This is where you are making a fatal mistake."

The above quotes were taken from Messenger Elijah Muhammad's book, Message To The Blackman In America, and it directly speaks to us in a very straightforward manner. We have been awe-struck by what we have been deceived into believing is power; namely, the white man's ability to drop bombs, shoot bullets, and launch satellites. Since we have been raised on such a continued show of destructive force, we subsequently have been conditioned to believe that there is nothing else capable of defeating the white race; however, if you would but study the scripture and God's Messenger, the Honorable Elijah Muhammad, you will come to see that there is a humanly build planet made and prepared for this day to destroy this world as we know it.

The Mother Plane, as envisioned by the prophet Ezekiel, taught to, and seen by the Honorable Elijah Muhammad, the Last Messenger of Allah, "is one of the greatest wonders of man, in making military weapons." "These signs would serve as a warning to us and what we may expect. And, as we see today, they are coming to pass."

Why has the white man of America been holding back the knowledge of sightings from his people and the American once-slave? What is it that he is trying to hide? Why is he still building more sophisticated weapons? If the cold-war is truly over, who are the new weapons for?

We are living in a time that many wonders are unfolding; as Messenger Elijah Muhammad teaches, "Since 1914 which was the end of the time given to the devils (white race) to rule the original people (Black Nation), man has been preparing for a final showdown in the skies. He has made a remarkable advancement in everything pertaining to a deadly destructive war in the sky, but Allah, the Best of Planners, having a perfect knowledge of His enemies, prepared for their destruction long ago even before they were created. Thanks to Allah, to whom eternal praise is due, Who came in the flesh and blood: He has been for more than seventy years making Himself ready for the final war."

If you cannot conceive of a New World, then chances are you will fight for the old; consequently, in addition to making a fatal mistake, you will be destroyed as well.

Take it or let it alone.

Nasir Makr Hakim,
Minister of Elijah Muhammad

SECRETARIUS - X

EZEKIEL'S WHEEL: MOTHER PLANE

Article No. 1
May 25, 1973

BATTLE IN THE SKY!

The Bible and Holy Qur'an, both books, refer to the final war between God and the devil that would be decided in the sky. The white race was given the authority and power and 6,000 years to rule us, the Black Nation of earth, but at the end of 6,000, years there would be a great time of trouble and a great display of the signs of this final war between God and the white race (the devil).

These signs would serve as a warning to us and what we may expect. And, as we see today, they are coming to pass. And, all of the other signs and prophecies of such signs appearing just around that time of the ending and destruction of the world of evil (the white race) and the displaying of these signs, as Jesus mentioned some in the Heavens and some on the earth; and the preparation to be made for a final battle between God and the devil.

The white man has conquered both land and sea travel. The sea used to serve as a barrier against him. But now the white man has conquered her. The white man now

THE MOTHER PLANE

can go over her surface in the worst of storms, and he can go through her with under-surface boats as well (submarines).

Now the white man has cast his eyes into space (the sky), to conquer it, and he is doing that. The white race, having knowledge of what they may expect today, they are spending billions of dollars on space travel. He has now brought the moon to him and seen some of the stars. The main thing I guess you are thinking is: Can he win against God, if God and His Prophets have foretold the outcome of this battle in the sky? It is impossible for the white race to win. What makes it impossible for them to win is because they have not the power of the forces of nature, while the power of the forces of nature is in the Hand of God making it impossible for the white man to win in a war of this sort.

The white man cannot win against the God on earth, so why waste billions of dollars to fight against the God Who Has Power Over The Heavens And Earth? Why all of this hurry to try to ascend into the Heavens for a close-up peek into the planets when you are destined to be defeated? Both books (Bible, Holy Qur'an) prophesy of a great defeat for you. The Holy Qur'an refers to the Heavens as being a "guarded canopy" and, warns you that they have a flame waiting for you.

Also, the Bible prophesies in Revelations (the last book of the Bible), that fire was used to destroy the white race after they ascended on the breath of the earth (air). So we see them going up on the breath of the earth daily. What is their plan for wanting to land on the moon since they know they cannot make the moon their home? The white man would have to continue to live off the earth's air (oxygen and hydrogen).

The earth would still have to produce all their food for them. So, it is useless to think of any planet other than the earth as a home for earth people. Then, why are they spending billions of dollars just to go and look at these planets, or to try to land people on the moon? What are their plans for Mars and Venus since they cannot live on these planets?

Do they think these planets serve as great fortifications of God and they could cast their bombs on these planets and destroy them? Or, do they fear attacks upon themselves coming from these planets?

No, this is not necessary. The white man is not that great in the eyes of God. The earth has all the weapons necessary to destroy the white man and the white man cannot leave the earth's surface unless it Pleases Allah (God). Allah Has Power over the very life veins of the body. Allah Has Power over the brain cells of our body.

Just what do they have in mind in wanting to go to the moon, since they cannot live there very long even if they get there? It is very expensive to feed and water people on the moon. Though quite a bit could be carried there, what do they have in mind?

Do they think that they could fight God from the moon? Just remember, the old Bible's prophecy: Thou may

THE MOTHER PLANE

ascend above the clouds into the Heavens, but yet I will bring thee down to the sides of Hell. Or, you may go on the bottom of the sea-and that they are doing today.

The Holy Qur'an further says that whenever God gets ready to destroy a people, He opens up the heavens for them and gives them the pleasure of what they seek or lust after. And, then He destroys them. The Holy Qur'an further prophecies that the Heavens would be open to this people and the veil of every secret would be removed. This prophecy does not mean that the white man will, after that, be able to win against God in a battle between them and God.

WWW.MEMPS.COM

EZEKIEL'S WHEEL BATTLE IN THE SKY!

Article No. 2
June 8, 1973

In the battle in the sky, it is scientifically clear that the Wheel, the Mother Plane, will be the victor due to the fact that nature has given anyone the advantage over the other, if the other is not able to produce the type of weapon that is needed to overcome the attack of that one (the enemy).

When the Prophet Ezekiel (Bible) saw this battle in the sky and saw the Wheel, the Mother Plane, that would be the victor, it has encouraged us, the Black Nation, to have confidence in the victory of that Wheel (Mother Plane).

When the Prophet Ezekiel saw the vision of this Wheel (Mother Plane), Ezekiel became a little excited in his words. Ezekiel said, "Oh, wheel. Oh, Wheel." The Saviour affirmed it. The Wheel, the Mother Ship, is one of the greatest wonders of man, in making military weapons. The Black Scientists knew at the time that they built the Mother Ship, that the Mother Ship and its well-trained crew would have to fight with her and the other Nations of the earth.

The well-trained crew of the Mother Ship, the Wheel, can dodge the enemy and make the enemy to look

THE MOTHER PLANE

for the Wheel, where the Wheel is not. As the word goes, the crew of the Wheel can elude the enemy, anywhere in the sky that this crew desires to elude them. When actual fighting has been declared against the armies of the Planet Earth, the enemy will never get near enough to do any harm to the Wheel. Actually, the Wheel, the Mother Ship, serves as a carrier for 1,500 deadly prepared planes with which to visit mankind on Planet Earth.

Do not look for the Wheel, the Mother Plane, because it is not out there for you to find it where you are looking for it. I am so happy that Allah (God) has prepared this unmatchable weapon to save us, the Black People! It carries supplies for the crew of this made Wheel-like Plane...it is something to marvel at! The battle in the sky!

As the Black Man has been on the Planet Earth for billions and trillions of years, and the Black Man has been here that long, and there is no doubt about it! Do you think that the Black Man will allow the made man (the white race) that has been on the Planet Earth for only 6,000 years, to out-wit the Black nation in any war whether it be physical or mental? If I was the white man I would just give up and not try to fight and old ancient people who were here before the white man's father (Yakub) thought of making the white race. There is plenty that we will be discussing about this Wheel in The Battle In The Sky!

WWW.MEMPS.COM

THE END OF THE WAR

Article No. 3
August 3, 1973

What can we expect at the end of the War...paradise or hell? See Bible, Dan. 9:26, 27. "...and at the end of the war desolations are determined...and that determined shall be poured upon the desolate." This is like saying do not expect healing ointment to be poured on the sore that has been made. You will not get healing ointment. Instead, you will get a worse sore. With trying to find a job for the unemployed soldiers who are returning from the war zone (if they have a chance to return) this will be one of the worst headaches for the government, that she has ever received.

With unemployment mounting so fast, it will create revolution. And everybody will want to divide the government up into pieces and every leader will want to grab a piece, for his part, to try to muster some kind of government, patterned after his own way of thinking.

Desolation... if we are going to suffer deprivation in a country that has been the pride of the nations, this will make it altogether worse, for everybody will be thinking about the way that they used to live, and the freedom and the privileges that they used to have. And this will make anger rise up in the midst.

THE MOTHER PLANE

What I am trying to show you is that the Prophet Daniel cannot be wrong, because this 'desolation that is determined to be poured on the most desolate,' is aimed at the place in which we now live. And just remember, that you cannot expect paradise, here when such condition of desolation is headed toward America. And since we cannot make Prophets' words, other than the truth, we expect this desolation, and we are receiving this desolation, now.

And the way to hasten such desolation is to confuse the heads of government. And if we see this confusion of the heads of government, as plain as the five (5) fingers on our hand-and if we have only on (1) finger on our hand, we can see that the government is confused and cannot find a way out, in peace with itself-daily and nightly, we see and hear what they are doing.

It is a confused time of the governments, of which the citizens look to, for guidance. And how can the head guide, if it is not at peace with itself? Everybody regrets talking about the woe that is heading toward America and the woe that is in America. But, America brought this woe upon herself, by not doing Justice to her Black slaves.

Allah (God) wants to pay America for her injustice to her lowly Black slave. Allah (God) is not bringing this woe on America because of her injustice to nations outside of America. He is paying America for her injustice to we, the poor Black man in America, the Black slave!

WWW.MEMPS.COM

America has not received much woe yet, for how she killed outright, the poor Black Man in the south (Georgia). America has hated her Black slave worse than she hates rattlesnakes. America has given her Black slave every evil and indecent name that she could think of while yet her Black slave has been her safety ground.

America does not want to admit to her trouble for her Black slave is still here. But, there will be no jobs for anybody. One calamity after another, befalling America. When she thinks that one calamity is going out, another is just entering! These constant calamities will continue until America is on her hands and knees admitting that Allah-u-Akbar (Allah is the Greatest).

Every prophesy of the prophets, prophesying of destruction, is aimed at America. This is dreadful and awful trouble that is Divinely focused at America. I say to you, my black Brothers and Black sisters, Seek refuge in Allah. Fly to Allah. Come Follow me. I ask you to help me, to help you. But, you would rather see your money fall dead in the white man's hands than to offer it to me to try to help make some bread out of the earth for you. Remember,"...the end of the war desolations are determined." Keep waiting with your disbelief and doubt. You shall soon come to know that what Elijah Muhammad, has said to you, is most certainly the truth!

THE MOTHER PLANE

WWW.MEMPS.COM

OH WHEEL
PART I
MESSENGER MUHAMMAD'S
ANALYSIS OF EZEKIEL'S WHEEL

Article No. 4
August 24, 1973

This is a continuation of the deadly Wheel Plane (the Mother Ship) that the Prophet Ezekiel had a vision of, in the 1st Chapter of the Book in the Bible, which is entitled by the name, Ezekiel.

It has been over 2,000 years since the revelation of the Book, entitled Ezekiel. In this article we are about to go into the analyzation of Ezekiel's vision of a great Wheel. (Bible) The Bible scholars are a little confused over an exact date of Ezekiel's vision of the Wheel. Some of the Bible scholars are actually doubtful whether or not, there was an Ezekiel, living or not. They arrive at their various conclusions concerning the Book of Ezekiel and whether or not he was a living prophet or whether the Book of Ezekiel is a vision of a Prophet, or not, because of the style of the writing, of the Book.

Ezekiel is called a Priest in the chapter 1, verse 3 (bible). In Ezekiel 1:1, Ezekiel said that he was by the river

THE MOTHER PLANE

Chebar, in the land of the chaldeans. Ezekiel refers to 'the spirit of the Lord,' and "the hand of the Lord..." being upon him.

In the same, chap. 1:4 (Bible) Ezekiel said that he looked, "...and behold, a whirlwind came out of the north, a great cloud, and a fire enfolding itself..." This fire that Ezekiel saw coming out of the north enfolding itself, cannot refer to anything other than the nations of the north being united together.

Ezekiel, Chap. 1:5: And out of the midst of the fire enfolding itself "...came the likeness of four living creatures." and the appearance of these four living creatures; "...they had the likeness of a man." Since there were four living creatures, Ezekiel, should have said that they had the likeness of 'men'. But, instead, Ezekiel said, "they had the likeness of a man." singling these four appearances, to be referring to one man. Ezekiel, Chap. 1:6; "And their feet were straight feet; and the sole of their feet was like the sole of a calf's foot:..." A calf has a split foot. "...and they (feet) sparkled like the colour of burnished brass."

As Ezekiel has reference to a man having a cattle-like foot, this would actually refer to the man's rate of speed of travel. A calf cannot travel very fast. And the split-hoof would show that Ezekiel is referring to a people who have not been able to move fast, due to their traveling being impeded by an unlike-natural way.

WWW.MEMPS.COM

If this has reference to a man, and the man has a calf-like or ox-like foot, this has reference to the slowness of the Black once-slave whose foot was shackled by his white slave-master, to keep the slave from running away from his master.

The striking of stones by the feet of animals have been known to give off sparkle, and this "sparkle like the colour of burnished brass." This shows that the treading of the man... wherever he treaded, the man produces valuable metal, like brass ore is smelted, made and used for the building of civilizations.

Ezekiel 1:8. And yet this man with animal-like feet has "...the hands of a man under their wings on their four sides; and they four had their faces and their wings." Ezekiel 1:9: "Their wings were joined one to another;..." If it is referring to the wings of a plane, then the analyzation is clear, even to being joined one (wing) to another (wing). There, Ezekiel (1:10) plainly ekes out to us something to give a better analysis of his vision, for he said, "As for the likeness of their faces, they four had the face of a man,..."

If Ezekiel is talking about a man, we can get onto the straight way of giving his vision some likeness to the people, because Ezekiel is not altogether talking about metal, wood, iron and animals. Ezekiel Chap. 1:10 shows we now have to go and change what's referring to other than man is really referring to man. Ezekiel also says that they had the "...face of a lion on the right side: and they four had the face of an ox on the left; and the four also had the face of an eagle."

THE MOTHER PLANE

O WHEEL
PART II
MESSENGER MUHAMMAD'S
ANALYSIS OF EZEKIEL'S WHEEL

Article No. 5
August 31, 1973

This description of the face means that the people and their character is like a lion, and their flight is like the flight of an eagle. the lion is the most fearless of all of the beasts of the jungle.

The lion is the most fearless of both animal and beast. And the people, the Black People, when once fear has been removed from them,-they take on the characteristics of a lion! As Ezekiel says here in Chap. 1:10, the four creatures had these faces:...the face of a lion, on the right side: and the face on the left side was like an ox.

Since the lion is fearless and quick, he can attack instantly. This is referring to the Black Man. And as 'his face is as an ox on the left side,' this refers to the strength of the Black Man, when it comes to his enemy.

The Black Man's enemy is said to be on his left side, because the enemy cannot be said to be on his right side.

THE MOTHER PLANE

His enemy must be on his left side, therefore, on the left side is where the Black Man needs force and strength with which to remove his enemy.

So, the Black Man is pictured as an ox on the left side, because he must be powerful enough on his left side to defend himself with strength and power. Ezekiel Chap. 1:11 says that the wings were pointed upward. This means that the black man has to go up in order to attack his enemy. 'The Battle In The Sky'...because the Black man and the enemy of the Resurrection will settle their differences in the air. Ezekiel foresaw this.

As you notice, Ezekiel Chap. 1:11 gives the description of these wings "...two wings of every one were joined one to another, and two covered their bodies."...having about six wings... these represent planes.

Ezekiel Chap. 1:12: "And they went every one straight forward: whither the spirit was to go, they went; and they turned not when they went." This means that the creatures were given certain orders and they did not disobey the orders that were given to them.

"...Whither the spirit was to go, they went." This means that where the True Spirit of God and His Word was intended to go to a people, these cherubims (angels) were the carriers of the Word. Ezekiel Chap. 1:13: Ezekiel said, "As for the likeness of the living creatures their appearance was like burning coals of fire, and like the appearance of lamps: it went up and down among the living creatures; (the people)." This fire going up and down among the living creatures (people) this refers to the anger of the creatures, for Ezekiel says here (Chap. 1:13) "...And out of the fire went forth lightning." This is true of nature.

But, as this lightning here, is from the living creatures (the people) it could refer to the swiftness of a bomb, which is like lightning. Ezekiel Chap. 1:13: "And the living creatures ran and returned as the appearance of flash of lightning." As they have swift ways of moving from the Wheel and into the Wheel and to the casement, then they are prepared to go in and out of the Wheel (Mother Plane) like lightning. For if he goes outside to drop a bomb, he must hasten himself away from where he dropped the bomb in order to keep the enemy from attacking him.

Ezekiel chap. 1:15 says: "...behold one wheel upon the earth by the living creatures, with his four faces." This four faces could represent the color of the people that the Wheel and its crew seeks to defend, as we have races Black, Brown, Yellow, and Red. These four are the major colors of the Black Man.

Ezekiel Chap 1:16 says that the Wheel "was as it were a Wheel in the middle of a Wheel." Ezekiel Chap. 1:17: This Wheel went upward "upon their four sides." This means that the Wheel could fly either way. On either side of the Wheel it could fly. Ezekiel Chap. 1:18: "As for their rings, they were so high that they were dreadful; and their rings were full of eyes round about them four."

THE MOTHER PLANE

This verse means that the knowledge of the four nations was like faces full of eyes, in every direction that you look at them you see faces with eyes.

O WHEEL
MOTHER OF PLANES
EZEKIEL'S WHEEL PART III

Article No. 6
September 7, 1973

These faces represent the four nations which make up the Black Man. It means that the Spirit of God is now covering the Nation of the Black Man. In every direction it is the Face of God, and the Spirit of God, moving into the people, the same as the spirit of Yakub, the maker of the white race (the devil), moved into all of his newborn creatures (people) that Yakub was grafting.

In Ezekiel's vision of the Wheel (Bible), the people on the Wheel were referred to as 'creatures' and every move by the Wheel and the people of the Wheel was of a swift movement and of a direction that was made by God Himself, for them.

And they had the Spirit of God in them. They are referred to as 'living creatures.' The limitation of their lives; their life span, is not mentioned. Ezekiel Chap. 1:19: "...and when the living creatures were lifted up from the earth, the wheels were lifted up." Ezekiel Chap. 1:20: "Whither so ever the spirit was to go, they went, thither was their spirit to go ; and the wheel were lifted up..." The wheels mentioned

THE MOTHER PLANE

here could even be referring to people. Wherever they (the Wheels, the people) went it was the Purpose of Allah (God).

We take the Spirit here to mean the Aims and Purpose of Allah and that faith for carrying out His Aims and Purpose, as we understand, from what we read of this Wheel. The Wheel is in fact a ship (plane) made like a wheel. And it is made for the Purpose of Allah (God) carrying out His Aim upon this world. This Wheel is by no means to be taken lightly! After the Wheel has done its work it will have made way for a New World to be built under the Eyes and Guidance of Allah (God).

The Wheel is so wonderful that even the prophet had to declare it in these words, "O Wheel, O Wheel" meaning that he is admiring his vision that he was receiving from Allah (God). The Wheel is the most wonderful and the most miraculous mechanical building of plane that has ever been imagined by man. The planes on this Wheel will be sent down, earthward, and are capable of destroying the world almost at once. The Wheel, (the Mother Plane) is capable of carrying many people in it! The wheel is 1/2 mile by 1/2 mile in size.

The Wheel is capable of sitting up above earth's atmosphere for a whole year before coming down into earth's atmosphere to take on more oxygen and hydrogen for the people who are on this plane (the Wheel). Oh she is a wonderful thing!

The planes that she uses to send earthward are so swift that they can make their flight and return their plane to the Wheel, the Mother Plane, almost like a flash of lightning. O Wheel! Think over it! After trillions of years should we let a baby, only six months old (6,000 years old) outwit us? This I say to those ignorant people of mine. I do not say this to the white man, for the white man knows, too.

But, it is our Black People who the white man is desirous to keep dumb to the Power of our God, Allah. But, think over it! If the Black Man created the heavens and the earth...AND THE BLACK MAN DID CREATE THE HEAVENS AND THE EARTH...then what man is fool enough to challenge the Black Man.

But, in a twinkling of an eye, Allah (God) can take away the heavens and the earth, not to think over few little people just made six days ago (6,000 years ago). O Wheel, the greatest most miraculous plane ever built. There never was such a plane made before this Wheel. There never was a need for such a plane before now.

You may wish Mr. Enemy that you could get a shot at the Wheel with your jet planes and other military weapons, but you should just go home and go to sleep. No one can harm this plane, the Wheel. They are going to fix you up first, before the Wheel ever comes into sight!

You cannot live on the moon, only just so long as your oxygen and hydrogen last you. The moon is about the closest platform that I know of, that you could probably try

THE MOTHER PLANE

to use. Venus and Mars...you cannot use Venus and Mars. The people on Mars will not let you light (land) on Mars. If they do let you land on Mars, they will be silly to do so.

You would like to see what the people on Mars look like. That is not, say, impossible. O WHEEL...the greatest mechanical defender, powered by the Spirit of Allah, to protect us, the Black People on the face of the earth.

THE NOISE OF THE WHEEL
PART IV
MESSENGER MUHAMMAD'S
ANALYSIS OF EZEKIEL'S WHEEL

Article No. 7
September 14, 1973

Because of the great and powerful work of this great Wheel, it lifts up wheels (people). This lifting of wheels could be referred to as small nations of the Black Man-nations who have been crushed by the wheel of enslavement, by the white slave masters.

Ezekiel, Chap. 1:21...the unity of the Wheel. "When those went, these went; and when those stood and when those were lifted up from the earth,..." Which means people to be lifted up to higher places of position in the human families of the earth. Ezekiel, Chap. 1:24...The great noise that Ezekiel said he heard, "And then they (the wheels) went, I heard the noise of their wings, like the noise of great waters, as the voice of the Almighty, the voice of speech,..." This gives us the knowledge that his is the work of the Almighty, in the Last Days-the work of lifting up the people who were under the foot of others. Ezekiel, Chap. 1:25..."And there was a voice from the firmament that was over their heads, when they stood..." Here, Ezekiel did not tell us what the Voice said. He did

THE MOTHER PLANE

not give us the answer. He only said that it was a Voice from the firmament.

INSIDE EZEKIEL'S WHEEL PART V

Article No. 8
September 21, 1973

We continue, from last week, the analysis of Ezekiel's Wheel. In Ezekiel, Chap. 1:25, the prophet Ezekiel described winged creatures that he saw. Do not be foolish enough to think that these creatures that Ezekiel describes and which he refers to as 'living creatures,' have feathery wings. They did not have feathery wings that they let down.

In this vision of the Wheel, or plane, this plane is built so unlike the other planes that we could call it a mystery Wheel to what we had heretofore known! Ezekiel, Chap. 1:26, "And above the firmament that was over their heads was a likeness of a throne, as the appearance of a sapphire stone: and upon the likeness of the throne was the likeness as the appearance of a man above upon it."

In Ezekiel's Vision, 'the Voice that he heard coming from the firmament that was over their heads,' this really is referring to the future of the work of Plane's Master. The Voice is the Voice of the Master of the Plane.

And the Voice is described as being above the Plane. If the Voice is heard above the Plane then what was the voice in, or on? Was this Voice on another plane or on

THE MOTHER PLANE

another Wheel? In verse 26 (Ezekiel, Chap. 1:26, Bible) Ezekiel describes seeing something above the Wheel, (Plane) in his vision something, a throne, as having the appearance of a sapphire stone. And upon this stone that was the likeness of a throne, was the likeness as the appearance of a man above it.

Ezekiel, Chap. 1:27, "And I saw the color of amber as the appearance of fire round about within it, from the appearance of his loins even upward, and from the appearance of his loins even downward, I saw as it were the appearance of fire, and it had brightness round about it."

Ezekiel, Chap. 1:28, "As the appearance of the bow (rainbow) that is in the cloud in the day of rain..." As Ezekiel says, with the appearance of a man with all of this science on him and the dividing of him-an upper and a lower part of him, he said, "It was as it were the appearance of fire..." from the first description of the Wheel. It teaches the reader that the Wheel is designed for war purposes.

The Wheel is one of the most mysterious wheels that the world has ever dreamed of, in the way of military science. I say military science. This is exactly what the Wheel is. It is a Wheel that is made to do military work.

By what Ezekiel said now, about the appearance of it, there is no doubt about the interpretation of this Wheel... that is military built, for war purposes, and that the Wheel is guided especially by the desire of God Almighty.

As we continue to analyze verse 28, Ezekiel describes the frightfulness of the Wheel as the appearance of "...the likeness of the glory of the Lord." This brings us into Divine Spirit of God in the making of the Wheel. So much proves the Wheel to be Divine Work, that Ezekiel, in the 28th verse, said that when he saw it, he fell upon his face... But, Ezekiel said that he 'heard a Voice of one that spake.'

Note how Ezekiel gives this to us, "One that spake." What One that speaks? We all speak! Ezekiel, Chap. 2:1, "And he said unto me, Son of man, stand upon thy feet, and I will speak unto thee." Here comes to us that a Divine Mission is going into the interpretation of the Plane (Wheel). Ezekiel adds, "...He said unto me. Son of man..."

This refers to a prophet of God are both in the Wheel taking it over. And God advises the Son of man (Prophet Ezekiel) to "stand upon his feet..." for in the verse above (Ezekiel, Chap. 1:28) Ezekiel said that he had 'fallen upon his face.'

The Spirit of God entered into Ezekiel and set him on his feet (Ezekiel, Chap. 2:2) This is the mission of the Prophet of God. And the God must make the Prophet who He has now missioned, aware of the protection against the enemy and the warring work that will be carried out, by the Wheel.

Ezekiel Chap. 2:3 says that Ezekiel is sent to "the children of Israel, to a rebellious nation..." Ezekiel, Chap. 2:3 describes them to be "impudent and stiff-headed." This

THE MOTHER PLANE

verse is referring to the Black People in America! But, the Black People in America must be warned whether they will hear or not. "They are a rebellious people" called 'a house' which means a nation (Ezekiel, Chap. 2:5).

They must be warned regardless to what type of people they may be. They must know the truth. "...yet shall know that there has been a prophet among them (Ezekiel, Chap. 2:5)." They (the Black People in America) must be warned as all of the People of God were warned the same. They are terrible people. They are dangerous people, as the prophet is warned, (Ezekiel, Chap. 2:6) "...be not afraid of them, neither be afraid of their words..." They speak stout words, disgraceful words, against the truth and the truth-bearer.

Ezekiel, Chap. 2:6 (continued), "...be not afraid of them, neither be afraid of their words, though briers and thorns be with thee, and thou dost dwell among scorpions: be not afraid of their words, nor be dismayed at their looks, though they be a rebellious house (nation).

It is the Black Man in America who is described here in this scripture. This is what he is. He is like scorpions where the Messenger of God (Prophet) is. This is a terrible thing, but you have proof of it here. He (The Messenger) is warned that he is living with people who are like a scorpion. A scorpion will sting and he will bite. A scorpion will do both. "Be not afraid of their words." They are always planning and saying evil and anonymous things against the Messenger.

WWW.MEMPS.COM

They look like they are very dangerous but the Messenger is not to be afraid of their looks. The Messenger must speak the words of God to them, whether they will hear, or whether they will forbear...(Ezekiel, Chap. 2:7). The Messenger is warning you, here is what God said to him.

Ezekiel, Chap. 2:8 tells the Messenger not to be rebellious "like that rebellious house (people): open your mouth and eat that I give thee! (What the mouth of the Lord give thee)." Ezekiel, (The Messenger) saw his mission coming to him in the roll of a book (Ezekiel, Chap. 2:10) "And he spread it before me; and it was written within and without: and there was written therein lamentations, and mourning, and woe (that went along with the book)."

The Messenger's mission here in Ezekiel, Chapters 2 and 3 is similar to the mission given to the Messenger in the Revelation of John, which refers to the bitterness and the sweetness, the good and the bad, of his mission. In Ezekiel, Chap. 3:5, God makes it clear to the Messenger "...thou are not sent to a people of strange speech and of an hard language, but to the house of Israel (to your own people)."

This portion of the "Wheel" is taken from "Message To The Blackman," pages 290-294 as follows, taught and written by the Honorable Elijah Muhammad, (PBUH). Certain words may be found to be alike in different places of his writings, but, in this, he is only making clear his explanation of the "Wheel."

The Mother Plane

BATTLE IN THE SKY IS NEAR

The vision of Ezekiel's wheel in a wheel in the sky is true if carefully understood. There is a similar wheel in the sky today which very well answers the description of Ezekiel's vision. This wheel corresponds in a way with the sphere of spheres called the universe. The Maker of the universe is Allah (God) the Father of the black nation which includes the brown, yellow, and red people. The Great Wheel, which many of us see in the sky today is not so much a wheel as one may think in such terms, but rather a place made like wheel. The like of this wheel-like plane was never seen before. You cannot build one like it and get the same results. Your brains are limited. If you would make one to look like it, you could not get it up off the earth into outer space. The similar Ezekiel's wheel is a masterpiece of mechanics. Maybe I should not say the wheel is similar to Ezekiel's vision of a wheel, but that Ezekiel's vision has become a reality. His vision of the wheel included hints on the Great Wisdom of Almighty God (Allah); that really He is the Maker of the universe, and reveals just where and how the decisive battle would take place (in the sky).

When guns and shells took the place of the sword, man's best defense against such weapons was a trench (ditch). Poison gas and liquid fire brought him out. Today, he has left the surface for the sky to destroy his enemy by dropping and exploding bombs on each other. All this was

THE MOTHER PLANE

known in the days of Ezekiel, and God revealed it to him, that through Ezekiel we might know what to expect at the end of this world.

The Originator and his people (the original black people) are supremely wise. Today, we see the white race preparing for the sky battle to determine who shall remain and rule the earth, black or white. In the battle between God and the disbelievers in the days of Noah, the victor's weapon was water. He used fire in the case of Sodom and Gomorrah. In the battle against Pharaoh, He used ten different weapons, which included fire and water, hail stones and great armies of the insect world and droughts and finally plagued them with death.

The Holy Qur'an says: "The chastisement of Pharaoh was like that which God would use against His enemies in the last days." Throughout the Bible and Holy Qur'an's teaching on the judgment and destruction of the enemies, fire will be used as the last weapon. The earth's greatest arms are fire and water. The whole of its atmosphere is made up of fire and water and gasses. It serves as a protected coat of arms against any falling fragments from her neighbors. Ezekiel saw a wheel in the middle of a wheel. This is true (the universe in the universe; it is made up of revolving spheres). There are wheels in the wheel.

The present wheel-shaped plane known as the Mother of Planes, is one-half mile by a half mile and is the largest mechanical man-made object in the sky. It is a small human planet made for the purpose of destroying the present

WWW.MEMPS.COM

world of the enemies of Allah. The cost to build such a plane is staggering! The finest brains were used to build it. It is capable of staying in outer space six to twelve months at a time without coming into the earth's gravity. It carries fifteen hundred bombing planes with most deadliest explosives-the type used in bringing up mountains on the earth. The very same method is to be used in the destruction of this world. The bombs are equipped with motors and the toughest of steel was used in making them. This steel drills and takes the bombs into the earth at a depth of one mile and is timed not to explode until it reaches one mile into the earth. This explosion produces a mountain one mile high; not one bomb will fall into water. They will all fall on cities. As Ezekiel saw and heard in his vision of it (Chapter 10:2) the plane is terrible. It is seen but do not think of trying to attack it. That would be suicide!

The small circular-made planes called flying saucers, which are so much talked of being seen, could be from this Mother Plane. This is only one of the things in store for the white man's evil world. Believe it or believe it not! This is to warn you and me to fly to our own God and people.

THE MOTHER PLANE

THE GREAT DECISIVE BATTLE IN THE SKY

And there shall be signs in the sun and in the moon and in the stars, and upon the earth distress of nations with perplexity; the sea and the waves roaring; men's hearts failing them for looking after those things which are coming on the earth: for the powers of heaven shall be shaken. They see the Son of Man coming in a cloud with power and great glory: (St. Luke 21:25-27).

You will bear me witness that we are living in such time as mentioned in the above prophecy-signs in the sun and in the moon. The phenomena going on in the sun and its family of planets testify to the truth that something of the greatest magnitude is about to take place. The final war or battle between God and the devils in the sky.

Allah (God), who has power over all things, is bringing the powers of the sun, moon and stars into display against His enemies. The fire of the sun to scorch and burn men and the vegetation and dry up the waters. The moon will eclipse her light to bring darkness upon man and upon man and upon all living things, to disrupt with her waves all air communications. The magnetic powers of the moon will bring about such tidal waves of seas and oceans as man has never witnessed before: the sea and the waves roaring.

THE MOTHER PLANE

As men's hearts fail them with fear at the sea, looking upon great tidal waves coming toward them like mounts, they also shall see such a great display of power from Allah (God) in the sky that their hearts will fail. Great earthquakes never felt before since man was upon the earth will take place, say the Bible and the Holy Qur'an. The Holy Qur'an says: "There will not be one city left that will not be leveled to the ground." Using this force against the enemies of Allah will make it impossible for them to survive.

This is all known to this world, but why are they trying to build up a defense against God. It is useless. America has it coming. Look how she has been and still is mistreating her freed slaves (so-called Negroes). The foolish (so-called) Negro preachers and leaders want social equality with these, their enemies. The great distress of nations spoken or prophesied of coming in the above chapter and verses is now going on. confusion, confusion all over the Western world today.

They (devils) see the end of their world and they see the signs of the Son of Man coming in the sky with power and great glory (the great Ezekiel's wheel and the unity of the Muslim world and the distress of nations).

The so-called Negro must awaken before it is too late. They think the white man's Christianity will save them regardless of what happens, and they are gravely mistaken. They must know that the white man's religion is not from God nor from Jesus or any other of the prophets. It is controlled by the white race and not by Almighty Allah (God).

"The near event draws nigh, there shall be none besides Allah to remove it. Do you wonder at this announcement? And will you laugh and not weep? While you sport and play, so make obeisance to Allah and serve Him" (Holy Qur'an 53:57, 58, 59, 60). Let us remember another Qur'an saying: "None disputes concerning the communications of Allah (God) but those who disbelieve, therefore let not their going to and fro in the cities deceive you. The people of Noah and the parties after them rejected prophets before them, and every nation purposed against their Apostle to destroy him and they disputed by means of the falsehood that they might thereby render null the truth. Therefore I destroyed them: how was then my retribution and thus did the word of your Lord prove true against those who disbelieved that they are the inmates of the fire" (Holy Qur'an 40:4-6).

THE MOTHER PLANE

THE BATTLE IN THE SKY

The final war between Allah (God) and the devils is dangerously close. The very least amount of friction can bring it into action within minutes. There is no such thing as getting ready for this most terrible and dreadful war; they are ready. Preparation of the battle between man and man or nations has been made and carried out on land and water for the past 6,000 years. Man has now become very wise and has learned many secrets of nature, which makes the old battle with swords, bows and arrows look like child's play.

Since 1914, which was the end of the time given to the devils (white race) to rule the original people (Black Nation), man has been preparing for a final showdown in the skies. He has made a remarkable advancement in everything pertaining to a deadly destructive war in the sky, but Allah, the Best of Planners, having a perfect knowledge of His enemies, prepared for their destruction long ago even before they were created. Thanks to Allah, to whom eternal praise is due, Who came in the flesh and the blood: He has been for more than seventy years making Himself ready for the final war.

Allah, whom we praise, comes in the person of Master W.F. Muhammad, the Great Mahdi, expected by the Muslims, and the anti-Christs (the devils) under the names : Son of Man, Jesus Christ, Messiah, God, Lord, Jehovah, the

THE MOTHER PLANE

Last (Jehovah) and the Christ. These meanings are good and befitting as titles, but the meaning of His name "Mahdi," as mentioned in the Holy Qur'an Sharrieff 22: 54, is better. All of these names refer to Him. His name, Fard Muhammad, is beautiful in its meaning. He must bring an end to war, and the only way to end war between man and man is to destroy the war-maker (the troublemaker).

According to the history of the white race (devils), they are guilty of making trouble, causing war among the people and themselves ever since they have been on our planet Earth. So, the God of the righteous has found them disagreeable to live with in peace, and has decided to remove them from the face of the Earth. God does not have to tell us that they are disagreeable to live with in peace; we already know it, for we are the victims of these trouble-makers. Allah will fight this war for the sake of His people (the black people), and especially for the American so-called Negroes. As I have said time and again, we the so-called American Negroes, will be the lucky ones. We are Allah's choice to give life and we will be put on top of civilization.

This next portion on the "Wheel," also written by Messenger Elijah Muhammad, was taken from "The Fall Of America," pages 236-242. As you continue to read this most factual, enlightening and only true explanation of the "Wheel," you will begin to know that Allah is truly God, and the Honorable Elijah Muhammad was, without a doubt, His last and greatest Messenger.

WWW.MEMPS.COM

THE MOTHER PLANE

The Mother Plane was made to destroy this world of evil and to show the wisdom and mighty power of the God Who came to destroy an old world and set up a new world.

The nature of the new world is righteousness. The nature of the new world cannot be righteousness, as long as unrighteousness is in its midst. The same type of plane was used by the Original God to put mountains on His planets.

Allah (God) Who came in the Person of Master Fard Muhammad, to Whom praises are due forever, is wiser than any god before Him as the Bible and the Holy Qur'an teach us. He taught me that this plane will be used to raise mountains on this planet (earth). The mountains that He will put on this earth will not be very high. He will raise these mountains to height of one (1) mile over the United States of America.

This reminds us of the prophet's prediction of this time of the destruction of the old world and the bringing in of new world: "Behold, the Lord, maketh the earth empty, and maketh it waste, and turneth it upside down, and scattereth abroad the inhabitants thereof." (Bible Is. 24:1).

There are planes in various nations today, but this is the mother of them all. Why? Because this type of plane

THE MOTHER PLANE

was used before the making of this world. Why should God make such a sign of His power to destroy a nation? Because this is the final destruction of that people who have opposed God in His purpose and aims for Justice and Righteousness.

The white race is not a people who were made righteous and then turned to unrighteousness; they were made unrighteous by the god who made them (Mr. Yakub).

Allah (God) Who came in the Person of Master Fard Muhammad, to Whom praises are due forever, taught me that this Plane is capable of reaching a height of forty miles above the earth. His words could have been seen meaning forty years, in which the Plane would go into action, and not referring actually to forty miles. Allah (God) does not speak one word that does not have meaning. Every word that He speaks has meaning.

The Mother Plane, according to what has been described of it by the devil scientists, is capable of not only staying up for periods of time; but it is also capable of eluding the scientists. They want to attack and destroy it; but if a plane did get close enough to attempt to carry out this purpose it would be destroyed instead. The white man has learned that this is not a plane to be played with. Planes come out of the Mother Plane.

The 1930's Canadian newspapers reported that they saw the Wheel (Mother Plane). It came down out of they sky. They admitted that it looked like a great city, and that something came down from it; it appeared to be a tube, but the tube-like thing went back up again.

Allah (God) Who came in the Person of Master Fard Muhammad, to Whom praises are due forever, taught me that after six months to a year, the Mother Plane comes into the gravity of the earth. It takes on oxygen and hydrogen in order to permit it to stay out of the earth's gravity until it needs refueling again.

THE MOTHER PLANE

EZEKIEL'S PROPHECY OF THE WHEEL

Ezekiel saw the Mother Plane in a Vision. According to the Bible, he looked up and saw this Plane (Ez. 1:16) and he called it a wheel, because it was made like a wheel. A plane that is wheel-shaped can turn in any direction, at any time. He admitted that the Plane was so high that it looked dreadful, and he cried out, "O wheel" (Ez. 10:13).

Ezekiel saw great work going on in the wheel and four living creatures "And their work was as it were a wheel in the middle of a wheel." (Ez. 1:16). And when the living creatures went, the wheels went with them: and when the living creatures were lifted up from the earth, the wheels, were lifted up Ez. 1:19. The power of the lifting up of the four creatures was in the wheel. The four creatures represents the four colors of the original people of the earth.

There are five great powers of the nations of the earth. These five Powers are the Black, Brown, Yellow, Red and white. Of the four Original Powers the Red is not an equal Power. The vision show the four creatures being lifted up from the earth. When the wheel was lifted up, they were lifted up and when the wheel stood, they stood. This means that they waited upon the movement of the wheel.

The Mother Plane

In Ezekiel's vision concerning the wheel, he said that he heard the voice of one tell the other to take coals of fire and to scatter it over the cities; this means bombs. It could mean fire too, however. The Plane is to drop bombs which would automatically be timed to burrow quickly to a position of one mile below the surface of the earth where they are timed to explode.

Allah (God) taught me that these bombs are not to be dropped into water. They are to be dropped only on the cities. It will be the work of the wheel. The wheel is the power of the four creatures, namely the four colors of the Black Man (black, brown, yellow and red). The red Indian is to benefit also from the judgment of the world.

We must remember that God comes to separate from the righteous that which is hindering the righteous from making progress and to destroy the effect of the poison of that which has opposed the righteous. The effect of the poison will be fully destroyed after the destruction of the source of the poison, which has poisoned the righteous.

It is like one being bitten by a rattlesnake. Quickly medication is administered in order to minimized the effect of the poison upon flesh and blood until a complete cure is effected; and then the patient recuperates and is well again.

It is useless to try to ignore Ezekiel's vision of the wheel, for the make and the destructive work of the wheel was foretold before it came to pass. The disbeliever believes that which he sees present and not that which is prophesied to come. That is why he is the loser and takes the course to hell, because he disbelieves in that which is prophesied to come about a particular day.

This is what the enemy is trying to do today with the Black Man. He is fascinating him with sport and play and indecency and the doing of evil to keep him from going to the God Who is present.

You never thought the day would come when you would see your wife, mother and old grey-haired women walking down the street today, half-nude. A few years ago they would not have dared to come out in the public like that. But now they do so, because the devil has put his approval on that kind of attire. They desire to please the devil. They do whatever the devil bids them to do. The devil desires to take the Black man with him to his doom.

Let us not classify the prophets as liars and ignore their prophecies of what may cause our self-destruction through belief in the devil instead of belief in the God of righteousness. There is no known equal of the Mother Plane. This is the reason why she is called the Mother Plane. The Mother Plane is made for the purpose of destroying the present world. She has no equal. Do not marvel at the make of this plane, since it is from the God Who made the universe of floating planets and stars, which are supported only by the Power of Allah in their rotation in their orbits.

Allah (God), Who came in the person of Master Fard Muhammad, to Whom praises are due forever, taught me

THE MOTHER PLANE

that the Mother Plane is a little human-made planet. Is it not simple for Allah (God) to make a new planet if He wants to? The Mother Plane is capable of staying out of the earth's gravity for a whole year. She is capable of producing her own sphere of oxygen and hydrogen, as any other planet is able to do. The Mother Plane carries the same type of bomb on her that our black scientists dropped on the planet earth to bring up mountains out of the earth after the planet earth was created.

The knowledge of how to do this has not been given to the world (white race), nor will they ever get this kind of knowledge. The knowledge of the world is limited. If the devil would get this type of knowledge, we could just say that we are goners. However, they are not able to attain this type of knowledge.

What does a six day old baby (white race) look like trying to compete with a six year old child (Black Nations)? For the six year old child can run all out in the yard and play. He can eat solid food. The power of the six-day-old baby is limited. The knowledge and power of this world's life (white race) is limited. The world of the white man was made from what he found and what he has seen and learned from the work of the original Black man. The white race is far from being able to equal the power and wisdom of the original Black man.

The Mother Plane and her work is a display of the power of the mightiest God, Master Fard Muhammad, to Whom praises are due forever. Master Fard Muhammad, to

Whom praises are due forever, is the Wisest and Best Knower; He is the Mightiest of Them All. "O wheel," says the prophet Ezekiel. She was so high up in the sky that she looked dreadful.

She is capable of staying away from you who plan the destruction of her. She is capable of confusing you who would try to reach her with your means of destruction. There are scientists on the Mother Plane who know what you are thinking about before the thought materializes (Holy Qur'an, ch. 50:16). Therefore, it is impossible to try to attack the Mother Plane. She can attack you, but you cannot attack her.

The Mother Plane can hide behind other stars and make herself invisible to the eye, because she does not have to wait on a power from the earth. She can produce her own power to go wherever she desires to go in space. The Mother Plane is not like your little bullets or cameras, which are powered by your limited power. The Bible prophecy's that today Allah (God) wishes to make known to us that He is God. He wishes to be respected as the superior God. He wishes all life in the universe to know that He is the greatest.

The Muslim recognizes Allah (God) to be the greatest. He always repeats "Thou are the Greatest. There is no God Like unto Thee, None deserves to be served or worshipped besides Thee." O mighty wheel. I repeat, that there is plenty of significance to the course of operation of her work. Space here in this book is limited, but what Allah

THE MOTHER PLANE

(God) taught me concerning the Mother Plane could be put into book-form.

O wheel, made to rock the earth and to heave up mountains upon the earth. O wheel, destroyer of nations. No wonder the prophet Isaiah prophesied that the "earth shall reel to and fro like a drunkard..."(Bible; Is. 24:24.) Let us seek refuge in Allah (God) from the destructive work to come from this Mother of planes.

WWW.MEMPS.COM

Thank you for purchasing this book. We trust the reading was rewarding and enlightening.

We offer various titles and a comprehensive collection of Messenger Elijah Muhammad's works. These works include:

- Standard Published Titles
- Unpublished & Diligently Transcribed Compilations
- Audio Cassettes
- Video Cassettes
- Audio CD's
- DVD's
- Rare Articles

You are welcomed to sample a listing of these items by simply requesting a FREE archive Catalog.

Our contact information is as follows:

Secretarius MEMPS Publications
111 E Dunlap Ave, Ste 1-217
Phoenix, Arizona 85020-7802
Phone & Fax 602 466-7347
Email: secmemps@gmail.com
Web: www.memps.com

Wholesale options are also available.

THE MOTHER PLANE

Printed in Great Britain
by Amazon